This book belongs to:

_____

GIANT PANDAS

by JILL ANDERSON

NORTHWORD
Minnetonka, Minnesota

In the misty mountains of China, a giant panda lumbers through a bamboo forest.

This bear's round head and furry body make it look as cuddly as a **teddy bear!**

It rolls and tumbles just for fun.

See its beautiful coat?
It has big black patches
around its eyes.

Its ears, legs and arms are

black, too. The rest is white.

Pandas are
gentle and shy,
and they like to be
alone.
The only time
they meet up with
other adult pandas is
at mating time.

Since pandas don't spend a lot of time together, they use scent messages to keep in touch.

By clawing, rubbing, or urinating on trees, they leave behind scents that tell each other, "I've been here" or "It's almost mating time!"

Pandas spend at least half of their day eating. What's on the menu? **Bamboo, bamboo,** and more **bamboo!**

A panda sits on its bottom and uses its front paws to eat.

Each paw has five fingers, plus an extra flap of skin and bone that works like a thumb to help the panda grasp its food.

Pandas use their strong teeth to crush the tough bamboo stems and strip off the leaves.

They wash down their leafy meals with lots of water.

When a mother panda
is ready to have a baby, she
makes a cozy den
in the base of a large tree
or in a cave. Her newborn
cub is no bigger than a
stick of butter!

At first, the panda cub is blind and helpless.

It cuddles up to its mother for warmth and milk.

Finally the cub's eyes open.
It is curious to
see what's
outside
the den.

Together, the mother panda and her cub play and feed.

In the cool evening,
they snuggle together,
dreaming of bamboo.

For Stuart,
who's more cuddly than any bear.
—J. A.

Composed in the United States of America
Designed by Lois A. Rainwater • Edited by Kristen McCurry

NorthWord
Books for Young Readers
11571 K-Tel Drive
Minnetonka, MN 55343
www.tnkidsbooks.com

Photographs © 2006 provided by:
Cyril Ruoso/JH Editorial/Minden Pictures: cover, pp. 6-7, 22-23; JupiterImages Corporation: back cover, pp. 2-3, 14, 24;
Gerry Ellis/Globio/Minden Pictures (http://info.globio.org): pp. 1, 4-5, 15, 21; istockphoto.com: pp. 8-9;
Pete Oxford/Minden Pictures: p. 10; Fritz Poelking/Alamy Images: p. 11; Michael Chen/istockphoto.com: p. 12;
Rob Friedman/istockphoto.com: p. 13; Digital Vision/Punchstock.com: pp. 16-17; Katherine Feng/Globio/Minden Pictures: pp. 19, 20.

Library of Congress Cataloging-in-Publication Data

Anderson, Jill.
Giant Pandas / by Jill Anderson.
p. cm. -- (Wild ones)
ISBN 1-55971-937-0 (hardcover) -- ISBN 1-55971-938-9 (softcover)
1. Giant panda--Juvenile literature. I. Title.

QL737.C214A53 2006

599.789--dc22

2005018644

Printed in Singapore
10 9 8 7 6 5 4 3 2 1